SCHIRMER'S LIBRARY
OF MUSICAL CLASSICS

Vol. 2006

JOHANN QUANTZ

Flute Concerto
In G Major

For Flute and Piano

ISBN 978-0-7935-3696-2

G. SCHIRMER, Inc.

DISTRIBUTED BY

HAL•LEONARD®
CORPORATION
7777 W. BLUEMOUND RD. P.O. BOX 13819 MILWAUKEE, WI 53213

Preface

Georges Barrère, one of the greatest flutists of all time, came to New York from Paris in May of 1905. No one in New York had ever heard a flutist play with such a beautiful tone, such virtuosity and artistry. Barrère created an immediate sensation and made a lasting impression. Within a year he had, perhaps unconsciously, completely revolutionized the New York flute world. He changed the concept of flute playing from the German style, which was the accepted norm at the time, to the lighter, more flexible and brilliant French style.

Barrère was brought to New York by conductor Walter Damrosch to be the first flute of his New York Symphony. However, Barrère was much more than a seasoned orchestral player. He was a dynamic and brilliant soloist who performed frequently with the Symphony both in New York and on tour. Barrère introduced his new style of flute playing and his artistry to countless flute players, many of whom came to New York to study with him.

I had the great privilege of studying with Georges Barrère for nine years. In 1933, while a student at the Juilliard School, I performed the Quantz Concerto in G Major with the Juilliard Orchestra. Barrère wrote these cadenzas for me at that time. I find them very beautiful, and am delighted to see them published here for the first time.

—FRANCES BLAISDELL

FLUTE CONCERTO
in G Major

I

Edited by Frances Blaisdell
with Cadenzas by Georges Barrère

Johann Joachim Quantz
(1697–1773)

-DE

II

Arioso e mesto

SCHIRMER'S LIBRARY
OF MUSICAL CLASSICS

Vol. 2006

JOHANN QUANTZ

Flute Concerto
In G Major

FLUTE

ISBN 978-0-7935-3696-2

G. SCHIRMER, Inc.

DISTRIBUTED BY

7777 W. BLUEMOUND RD. P.O. BOX 13819 MILWAUKEE, WI 53213

FLUTE CONCERTO
in G Major

I

Edited by Frances Blaisdell
with Cadenzas by Georges Barrère

Johann Joachim Quantz
(1697 – 1773)

Flute

Flute

II

8

Flute

III

CADENZA